WANNA BE
SMILED AT?

by Bil Keane

FAWCETT GOLD MEDAL • NEW YORK

A Fawcett Gold Medal Book
Published by Ballantine Books

ISBN 0-449-12816-4

This edition published by arrangement with
The Register & Tribune Syndicate, Inc.

Manufactured in the United States of America

First Fawcett Gold Medal Edition: July 1970
First Ballantine Books Edition: March 1985

"Today's Saturday. Daddy left his whiskers on."

"Shall I bring PJ out? He's just wasting those pretty smiles in here all by himself."

"PJ tastes good when you kiss him. He just had banana pudding."

"They'd never let HIM stay in our school without a haircut."

"I passed them around and they all TOOK some!"

"Is it time for me to go to Greg's party, yet?"

"I'm waiting for Jeffy to come out. He couldn't read the signs so I told him which one to go into."

"When we're at Grandma's she always puts WARM
milk on our cereal!"

"Mommy! Tell PJ to stop hitting me. He's hurting my feelings."

"I was just feelin' to see if the juice is all mixed."

"Our hands and feet are cold but maybe some
hot chocolate would warm them up."

"That's not a choo-choo, Daddy. It's a DIESEL."

"The cleaners down the street always give
us lollipops."

"Won't Mommy be surprised when she sees we cleared the table for her?"

"Hi, Grandma! Did you get our letter?"

"PJ's taking a whole crowd of cookies!"

"Mommy! It's a commercial!"

"What do you want us to help you with after
we make the beds, Mommy?"

"No, your Super Space Capsule from the Flakies
Company did not arrive yet!"

"Give up, Daddy?"

"No fair comin' up that way, PJ! Get in line
like everybody else!"

"Poor Mommy. She never gets a dollar
in her card from Grandma."

"But, Mommy! How do you KNOW you have
everything you want for your birthday? You
haven't even opened your presents yet!"

"If you leave them up just one more week,
Daddy, we could turn them on for Easter!"

"Did Daddy say it was okay for you to use his tools?"

"The Easter Bunny prints just like Santa."

"If anybody wants me and can't find me, I'll be in my room playing my drum."

"Mommy! I just swept that part!"

"It has AM, FM, and UHF."

"They're spelling it 'cause we're here."

"Thank you for the pretty dress, Grandma. And Mommy said if you ask me if it fits I should say yes."

"Aunt Tess, what ever happened to your other friend
--the one who was going to be our Uncle TED?"

"It's pretty, Aunt Tess—It's just like the one
Dolly got out of the gum machine."

"How can you be in a WEDDING, Mommy?
Aren't you already married?"

"I am NOT being a flower child! I'm a flower GIRL!"

"Are you sure Dolly isn't getting married?"

"Stop lookin' happy, Billy. I think we're
supposed to cry."

"THROW the rice, PJ! Don't eat it!"

"Nobody gave them TOYS."

"Didn't Aunt Tess like those flowers she was carrying?"

"Flower girls never go on the honeymoon."

"The part of the wedding I liked best was where
Daddy kept blowing the car horn."

"Billy's catching all MY lightning bugs!"

"I forgot. I just don't have a good remembery."

"Where's PJ? Where's Barfy? They're missing all the pretty fireworks."

"Grandma told me to put this in the ice box.
What's an ice box?"

"Jeffy! You better put some of that back before
Mommy sees it!"

"Mommy, why don't you ever go jogging with Daddy to get some exercise?"

"I wish today was somebody's birthday. I feel
like eating some cake."

"Quick, Mommy! I need a jar with holes in the lid!"

"Oooo! I've been sitting on this leg and now my foot feels like ginger ale!"

"Mommy! The clock in your bedroom is ringing!
Should I answer it?"

"Know what I was doing over at Tommy's house today? Playing in his sandbox."

"Look how happy PJ's toes are when you feed
him ice cream."

"Mommy! Barfy's drinking up all of our water!"

"Look at the cute little green apple I found on
our tomato plant!"

"Daddy! Didn't you bring back sodas for us?"

"I want to take my nap sittin' up today, okay?"

"I made the ice cubes, Daddy. Aren't I a
good cook?"

"Now, how will Mommy know where I am?"

"The game wasn't so hot. In the top half of the
sixth they ran out of sodas."

"You can't play it, Dolly! You'll get my germs!"

"I can't find my shoe, Mommy, but I'm sure finding
a lot of other things under here."

"Mommy, would you please stand in front of the
window so the sun won't shine in my eyes?"

"I'd like you to meet my Mommy--MY WIFE!"

"PJ's not bein' kind to animals!   He stepped on
all my ants!"

"It hurts when Daddy hugs me while he's
wearing some pens."

"Big hand's on twelve, little hand's on five.
Time for cartoons on Channel Ten!"

"Mommy, what will my last name be when I get married?"

"Daddy! You left this money on the table!"

"The doctor hits you on the knee to see if your shoe will stay on."

"...and I'll need a bag to carry my A-B-C's in."

"Why can't I go to school, too?"

". . .and I know some of my ABC's, and I can count to fifty, and I know my zip code, and I can do the pledge of 'legiance. . ."

"Know what we did in school today? We glued!"

"The tooth fairy forgot again!"

"Mommy, will you tell Mr. Horton that the
saucer from my tea set isn't an ash tray?"

"Mommy! I think I
broke my little
heart!"

"Yes, Daddy--Mommy's here. She's lying down."

"Now can you go back and read us the words you
hopped over?"

"Mommy, has PJ had his din...oh yeah--he has."

"I peeled all the bananas for next week's lunches!"

"Mommy must really mean business. She called
the boys William and Jeffrey."

"Look! Barfy thinks his tail is ALIVE!"

"I know why the car pool's so late, Mommy! This is OUR morning to drive!"

"WATCH, EVERYBODY! OUR DADDY'S
GOING TO ROLL THE BALL!"

"What do you want to watch, Grandma--Atom Ant
or Bozo the Clown?"

"Mommy! That's not the lever Daddy pushed!"

"Mommy had to go buy herself a new dress today
'cause you saw her other one at the last party."

"Wave bye-bye to Grandma, PJ--come on,
love, please! Wave bye-bye..."

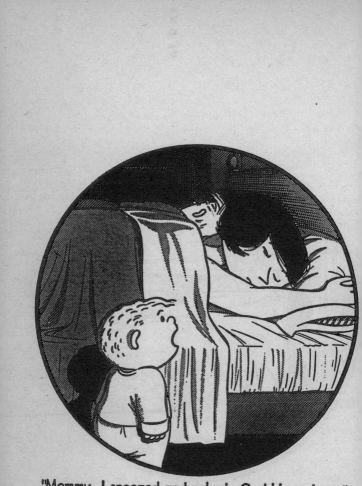

"Mommy, I sneezed and nobody God blessed me."

"Don't worry about your cut hand, Mommy. I'll
kiss it and make it better."

"Naughty broken glass! You cut Mommy's hand!"

"Mommy cut her hand and we have to take her to the doctor's."

"If you try not to cry, Mommy, the doctor might give us all lollipops."

"'Member your sore hand, Mommy! 'Member your
sore hand!"

"It needs more on it, Daddy. I can still see the bread."

"You close your eyes and count while I go hide
in the bathroom behind the door."

"Mommy, when other kids are around could you
call me Bill instead of Billy?"

"Pick me up, Daddy? I want to be up there
with you for a while."

"Do my whiskers hurt a lot, Mommy?"

"Our class is havin' a bake sale and I have to bring in 12 cupcakes and a dime to buy one of them "

"Mommy! Barfy won't 'scuse me."

"How do you KNOW you won't like it? You've
never even TASTED it!"

"Mommy, how many fingers old am I?"

"Mommy can tie it from the front."

"When I grow up and be a mommy, I'm only gonna have GIRLS!"

"You're coming to the kissing part."

"You can't play, PJ, 'cause we always have to
let you win."

"That's not dirt under my fingernails. It's peanut butter."

"Mommy, how do you make an 'A' and a 'B'?
I'm teaching PJ how to write."

"I'm making a copy of my letter to Santa to send to Grandma."

"Mommy! Wait for me!"

"Dasher, Dancer, Donner...let's see...Dasher, Dancer, PRANCER, Donner..."

"I want to buy this for my daddy. Do I have
enough money?"

"Gold, frankincense and myrrh? Why didn't they
bring Baby Jesus some toys?".

"Mommy! Can't we help you wrap some presents?"

"A go-cart with a three horsepower engine and
rear wheel brakes, and..."

"Remember, Barfy—bark real loud when Santa
comes so we can wake up."

"If you open it up, Grandma, you'll find out
it's soap."

"Billy's fixing my doll carriage and I haven't
even broken it yet!"

"Boy! You should see all the neat stuff Kevin
got for Christmas!"

"When CAN I carry him? He used to be 'too
little', and now you say he's 'too big'!"

"Daddy! Didn't you bring back sodas for us?"

They might run out of
gas . . . but never out of
laughs. You get plenty
of mirthful mileage on
this trip with

12816

0

27778 00225

ISBN 0-449-12816-4

P8-AFE-431